THE

YALE SERIES OF YOUNGER POETS

EDITED BY STEPHEN VINCENT BENÉT

FOR MY PEOPLE

D1073291

For My People

BY

MARGARET WALKER

WITH A FOREWORD BY

STEPHEN VINCENT BENÉT

NEW HAVEN

YALE UNIVERSITY PRESS

Centenary Edition, 2019

Published with assistance from a grant to honor James Merrill.
Originally published in 1942 by Yale University Press.

Yale University Press books may be purchased in quantity for
educational, business, or promotional use. For information,
please e-mail sales.press@yale.edu (U.S. office) or sales@yaleup.
co.uk (U.K. office).

Printed in the United States of America.

Library of Congress Control Number: 2019944097
ISBN 978-0-300-24640-7 (paperback : alk. paper)

A catalogue record for this book is available from the British
Library.

Some of these poems first appeared in *Poetry, a Magazine of
Verse*; *Opportunity, a Journal of Negro Life*; *Creative Writing*;
and *American Prefaces*.

This paper meets the requirements of ANSI/NISO Z39.48-1992 Per-
manence of Paper).

10 9 8 7 6 5 4 3 2 1

FOREWORD

"... For my playmates in the clay and dust and sand of Alabama backyards playing baptizing and preaching and doctor and jail and soldier and school and mama and cooking and playhouse and concert and store and hair and Miss Choomby and company;

For the cramped bewildered years we went to school to learn to know the reasons why and the answers to and the people who and the places where and the days when, in memory of the bitter hours when we discovered we were black and poor and small and different and nobody cared and nobody wondered and nobody understood;

. . . . .

For my people thronging 47th Street in Chicago and Lenox Avenue in New York and Rampart Street in New Orleans, lost disinherited dispossessed and happy people filling the cabarets and taverns and other people's pockets needing bread and shoes and milk and land and money and something—something all our own; . . ."

It is unfair to pick three verses out of a connected and powerful poem—the title poem of this book. Yet they do give the reader a taste of Miss Walker's quality. You will have to read the whole poem to know its whole impact—and you should do that.

Straightforwardness, directness, reality are good things to find in a young poet. It is rarer to find them combined with a controlled intensity of emotion and a language that, at times, even when it is most modern, has something of the surge of biblical poetry. And it is obvious that Miss Walker uses that language because it comes naturally to her and is part of her inheritance. A contemporary writer, living in a contemporary world, when she speaks of and for her people older voices are mixed with hers—the voices of Methodist forebears and preachers who preached the Word, the anonymous voices of many who lived and were forgotten and yet out of bondage and hope made a lasting music. Miss Walker is not merely a sounding-board for these voices—I do not mean that. Nor do I mean that this is interesting and moving poetry because it was written by a Negro. It is too late in the day for that sort of meaningless patronage—and poetry must exist in its own right. These poems keep on talking to you after the book is shut because, out of deep feeling, Miss Walker has made living and passionate speech.

"We Have Been Believers," "Delta," "Southern Song," "For My People"—they are full of the rain and the sun that fall upon the faces and shoulders of her people, full of the bitter questioning and the answers not yet found, the pride and the disillusion and the reality. It is difficult for me to read these poems unmoved—I think it will be difficult for others. Yet it is not only the larger problems of her "playmates in the clay and dust" that interest Margaret Walker—she is interested in people wherever they are. In the second section of her book you will find ballads and portraits—figures of legend, like John Henry and Stagolee and the uncanny Molly Means—figures of realism like Poppa Chicken and Teacher and Gus, the Lineman, who couldn't die—figures "of Old Man River, round New Orleans, with her gumbo, rice, and good red beans." They are set for voice and the blues, they could be sung as easily as spoken. And, first and last, they are a part of our earth.

Miss Walker can write formal verse as well; she can write her own kind of sonnet. But, in whatever medium she is working, the note is true and unforced. There is a deep sincerity in all these poems—a sincerity at times disquieting. For this is what one American has found and seen—this is the song of her people, of her part of America. You cannot deny its honesty, you cannot deny its candor. And this is not far away or long ago—this is part of our nation, speaking.

I do not know what work Miss Walker will do in the future, though I should be very much surprised if this book were all she had to give. But I do know that, in this book,

6

she has spoken of her people so that all may listen. I think that is something for any poet to have done.

Margaret Walker was born in Birmingham, Alabama, July 7, 1915. Her father is a Methodist minister, her mother a teacher of music. Both are university graduates. She has two sisters and a brother. Her early education took place in various church schools in Meridian, Mississippi; Birmingham, Alabama; and New Orleans, Louisiana. In 1935 she graduated from Northwestern University. For the next four years she worked in Chicago at various jobs—as typist, newspaper reporter, editor of a short-lived magazine, and on the Federal Writers Project. In 1939 she entered the School of Letters of the University of Iowa and received the degree of Master of Arts in 1940. She is now Professor of English at Livingstone College, Salisbury, North Carolina. She has written since she was thirteen, but *For My People* is her first published book.

STEPHEN VINCENT BENÉT

CONTENTS

III

Part One

FOR MY PEOPLE

For my people everywhere singing their slave songs repeat-
    edly: their dirges and their ditties and their blues and
    jubilees, praying their prayers nightly to an unknown
    god, bending their knees humbly to an unseen power;

For my people lending their strength to the years, to the gone
    years and the now years and the maybe years, washing
    ironing cooking scrubbing sewing mending hoeing
    plowing digging planting pruning patching dragging
    along never gaining never reaping never knowing and
    never understanding;

For my playmates in the clay and dust and sand of Alabama
    backyards playing baptizing and preaching and doc-
    tor and jail and soldier and school and mama and
    cooking and playhouse and concert and store and hair
    and Miss Choomby and company;

For the cramped bewildered years we went to school to learn
    to know the reasons why and the answers to and the
    people who and the places where and the days when,
    in memory of the bitter hours when we discovered we
    were black and poor and small and different and
    nobody cared and nobody wondered and nobody
    understood;

For the boys and girls who grew in spite of these things to be
    man and woman, to laugh and dance and sing and
    play and drink their wine and religion and success, to
    marry their playmates and bear children and then die
    of consumption and anemia and lynching;

For my people thronging 47th Street in Chicago and Lenox
    Avenue in New York and Rampart Street in New
    Orleans, lost disinherited dispossessed and happy

people filling the cabarets and taverns and other people's pockets needing bread and shoes and milk and land and money and something—something all our own;

For my people walking blindly spreading joy, losing time being lazy, sleeping when hungry, shouting when burdened, drinking when hopeless, tied and shackled and tangled among ourselves by the unseen creatures who tower over us omnisciently and laugh;

For my people blundering and groping and floundering in the dark of churches and schools and clubs and societies, associations and councils and committees and conventions, distressed and disturbed and deceived and devoured by money-hungry glory-craving leeches, preyed on by facile force of state and fad and novelty, by false prophet and holy believer;

For my people standing staring trying to fashion a better way from confusion, from hypocrisy and misunderstanding, trying to fashion a world that will hold all the people, all the faces, all the adams and eves and their countless generations;

Let a new earth rise. Let another world be born. Let a bloody peace be written in the sky. Let a second generation full of courage issue forth; let a people loving freedom come to growth. Let a beauty full of healing and a strength of final clenching be the pulsing in our spirits and our blood. Let the martial songs be written, let the dirges disappear. Let a race of men now rise and take control.

DARK BLOOD

There were bizarre beginnings in old lands for the making of me. There were sugar sands and islands of fern and pearl, palm jungles and stretches of a never-ending sea.

There were the wooing nights of tropical lands and the cool discretion of flowering plains between two stalwart hills. They nurtured my coming with wanderlust. I sucked fevers of adventure through my veins with my mother's milk.

Someday I shall go to the tropical lands of my birth, to the coasts of continents and the tiny wharves of island shores. I shall roam the Balkans and the hot lanes of Africa and Asia. I shall stand on mountain tops and gaze on fertile homes below.

And when I return to Mobile I shall go by the way of Panama and Bocas del Toro to the littered streets and the one-room shacks of my old poverty, and blazing suns of other lands may struggle then to reconcile the pride and pain in me.

WE HAVE BEEN BELIEVERS

We have been believers believing in the black gods of an old land, believing in the secrets of the seeress and the magic of the charmers and the power of the devil's evil ones.

And in the white gods of a new land we have been believers believing in the mercy of our masters and the beauty of our brothers, believing in the conjure of the humble and the faithful and the pure.

Neither the slavers' whip nor the lynchers' rope nor the bayonet could kill our black belief. In our hunger we beheld the welcome table and in our nakedness the glory of a long white robe. We have been believers in the new Jerusalem.

We have been believers feeding greedy grinning gods, like a Moloch demanding our sons and our daughters, our strength and our wills and our spirits of pain. We have been believers, silent and stolid and stubborn and strong.

We have been believers yielding substance for the world. With our hands have we fed a people and out of our strength have they wrung the necessities of a nation. Our song has filled the twilight and our hope has heralded the dawn.

Now we stand ready for the touch of one fiery iron, for the cleansing breath of many molten truths, that the eyes of the blind may see and the ears of the deaf may hear and the tongues of the people be filled with living fire.

Where are our gods that they leave us asleep? Surely the priests and the preachers and the powers will hear. Surely now that our hands are empty and our hearts too full to pray they will understand. Surely the sires of the people will send us a sign.

We have been believers believing in our burdens and our demigods too long. Now the needy no longer weep and pray; the long-suffering arise, and our fists bleed against the bars with a strange insistency.

SOUTHERN SONG

I want my body bathed again by southern suns, my soul
reclaimed again from southern land. I want to rest
again in southern fields, in grass and hay and clover
bloom; to lay my hand again upon the clay baked by
a southern sun, to touch the rain-soaked earth and
smell the smell of soil.

I want my rest unbroken in the fields of southern earth;
freedom to watch the corn wave silver in the sun and
mark the splashing of a brook, a pond with ducks
and frogs and count the clouds.

I want no mobs to wrench me from my southern rest; no
forms to take me in the night and burn my shack and
make for me a nightmare full of oil and flame.

I want my careless song to strike no minor key; no fiend to
stand between my body's southern song—the fusion
of the South, my body's song and me.

SORROW HOME

My roots are deep in southern life; deeper than John Brown
or Nat Turner or Robert Lee. I was sired and weaned
in a tropic world. The palm tree and banana leaf,
mango and cocoanut, breadfruit and rubber trees
know me.

Warm skies and gulf blue streams are in my blood. I belong
with the smell of fresh pine, with the trail of coon,
and the spring growth of wild onion.

I am no hot-house bulb to be reared in steam-heated flats
with the music of "L" and subway in my ears, walled
in by steel and wood and brick far from the sky.

I want the cotton fields, tobacco and the cane. I want to walk
along with sacks of seed to drop in fallow ground.
Restless music is in my heart and I am eager to be
gone.

O Southland, sorrow home, melody beating in my bone and
blood! How long will the Klan of hate, the hounds
and the chain gangs keep me from my own?

DELTA

I

I am a child of the valley.
Mud and muck and misery of lowlands
are on thin tracks of my feet.
Damp draughts of mist and fog hovering over valleys
are on my feverish breath.
Red clay from feet of beasts colors my mouth
and there is blood on my tongue.

I go up and down and through this valley
and my heart bleeds with my blood here in the valley.
My heart bleeds for our fate.
I turn to each stick and stone, marking them for my own;
here where muddy water flows at our shanty door
and levees stand like a swollen bump on our backyard.

I watch rivulets flow
trickling into one great river
running through little towns
through swampy thickets and smoky cities
through fields of rice and marshes
where the marsh hen comes to stand
and buzzards draw thin blue streaks against evening sky.
I listen to crooning of familiar lullabies;
the honky-tonks are open and the blues are ringing far.
In cities a thousand red lamps glow,
but the lights fail to stir me
and the music cannot lift me
and my despair only deepens with the wailing
of a million voices strong.

O valley of my moaning brothers!
Valley of my sorrowing sisters!
Valley of lost forgotten men.

O hunted desperate people
stricken and silently submissive
seeking yet sullen ones!
If only from this valley we might rise with song!
With singing that is ours.

II

Here in this valley of cotton and cane and banana wharves
we labor.
Our mothers and fathers labored before us
here in this low valley.

High above us and round about us stand high mountains
rise the towering snow-capped mountains
while we are beaten and broken and bowed
here in this dark valley.

The river passes us by.
Boats slip by on the edge of horizons.
Daily we fill boats with cargoes of our need
and send them out to sea.

Orange and plantain and cotton grow
here in this wide valley.
Wood fern and sour grass and wild onion grow
here in this sweet valley.

We tend the crop and gather the harvest
but not for ourselves do we labor,
not for ourselves do we sweat and starve and spend
under these mountains we dare not claim,
here on this earth we dare not claim,
here by this river we dare not claim.
Yet we are an age of years in this valley;
yet we are bound till death to this valley.

Nights in the valley are full of haunting murmurings
of our musical prayers
of our rhythmical loving
of our fumbling thinking aloud.
Nights in the houses of our miserable poor
are wakeful and tormenting,
for out of a deep slumber we are 'roused
to our brother who is ill
and our sister who is ravished
and our mother who is starving.
Out of a deep slumber truth rides upon us
and we wonder why we are helpless
and we wonder why we are dumb.
Out of a deep slumber truth rides upon us
and makes us restless and wakeful
and full of a hundred unfulfilled dreams of today;
our blood eats through our veins with the terrible destruction
of radium in our bones and rebellion in our brains
and we wish no longer to rest.

III

Now burst the dams of years
and winter snows melt with an onrush of a turbulent spring.
Now rises sap in slumbering elms
and floods overwhelm us
here in this low valley.
Here there is a thundering sound in our ears.
All the day we are disturbed;
nothing ever moved our valley more.
The cannons boom in our brains
and there is a dawning understanding
in the valleys of our spirits;
there is a crystalline hope
there is a new way to be worn and a path to be broken
from the past.

Into our troubled living flows the valley
flooding our lives with a passion for freedom.
Our silence is broken in twain
even as brush is broken before terrible rain
even as pines rush in paths of hurricanes.
Our blood rises and bursts in great heart spasms
hungering down through valleys in pain
and the storm begins.
We are dazed in wonder and caught in the downpour.
Danger and death stalk the valley.
Robbers and murderers rape the valley
taking cabins and children from us
killing wives and sweethearts before us
seeking to threaten us out of this valley.

Then with a longing dearer than breathing
love for the valley arises within us
love to possess and thrive in this valley
love to possess our vineyards and pastures
our orchards and cattle
our harvest of cotton, tobacco, and cane.
Love overwhelms our living with longing
strengthening flesh and blood within us
banding the iron of our muscles with anger
making us men in the fields we have tended
standing defending the land we have rendered
rich and abiding and heavy with plenty.

We with our blood have watered these fields
and they belong to us.
Valleys and dust of our bodies are blood brothers
and they belong to us:
the long golden grain for bread
and the ripe purple fruit for wine
the hills beyond for peace
and the grass beneath for rest

the music in the wind for us
the nights for loving
the days for living
and the circling lines in the sky
for dreams.

We are like the sensitive Spring
walking valleys like a slim young girl
full breasted and precious limbed
and carrying on our lips the kiss of the world.
Only the naked arm of Time
can measure the ground we know
and thresh the air we breathe.
Neither earth nor star nor water's host
can sever us from our life to be
for we are beyond your reach O mighty winnowing flail!
infinite and free!

LINEAGE

My grandmothers were strong.
They followed plows and bent to toil.
They moved through fields sowing seed.
They touched earth and grain grew.
They were full of sturdiness and singing.
My grandmothers were strong.

My grandmothers are full of memories
Smelling of soap and onions and wet clay
With veins rolling roughly over quick hands
They have many clean words to say.
My grandmothers were strong.
Why am I not as they?

SINCE *1619*

How many years since 1619 have I been singing Spirituals?
How long have I been praising God and shouting hallelu-
  jahs?
How long have I been hated and hating?
How long have I been living in hell for heaven?

When will I see my brother's face wearing another color?
When will I be ready to die in an honest fight?
When will I be conscious of the struggle—now to do or die?
When will these scales fall away from my eyes?

What will I say when days of wrath descend:
When the money-gods take all my life away;
When the death knell sounds
And peace is a flag of far-flung blood and filth?

When will I understand the cheated and the cheaters;
Their paltry pittances and cold concessions to my pride?
When will I burst from my kennel an angry mongrel,
Lean and hungry and tired of my dry bones and years?

PEOPLE OF UNREST

Stare from your pillow into the sun.
See the disk of light in shadows.
Watch day growing tall.
Cry with a loud voice after the sun.
Take his yellow arms and wrap them round your life.
Be glad to be washed in the sun.
Be glad to see.
People of unrest and sorrow
Stare from your pillow into the sun.

TODAY

I

I sing of slum scabs on city faces, scrawny children scarred by bombs and dying of hunger, wretched human scarecrows strung against lynching stakes, those dying of pellagra and silicosis, rotten houses falling on slowly decaying humanity.

I sing of Man's struggle to be clean, to be useful, to be free; of need arising from our lives, of bitter living flowing in our laughter, of cankerous mutiny eating through the nipples of our breasts.

I sing of our soon-to-be-dead, of last escape: drunkard raising flasks to his lips never tasting the solace, gambler casting his last die never knowing the win, lover seeking lips of the beloved never tasting fruit of his kiss, never knowing the languorous sleep.

I sing these fragments of living that you may know by these presents that which we feared most has come upon us.

II

You walking these common neighboring streets with no disturbing drone of bombing planes, no Sunday air-raiding, and no shells caving in roofs of your houses; fearing no severed baby arms nor naked eyeballs hurtled in your hands; riding trolley and jitney daily, buying gas and light hourly, viewing weekly "Wild West Indian and Shooting Sam," "Mama Loves Papa," and "Gone by the Breeze," complacently smug in a snug somnolescence;

You in Middle America distantly removed from Middle Europe, no closer than morning headlines and evening news flashes, bothered by petty personals —your calories and eyemaline, your henna rinse and dental cream, washing your lives with pity, smoothing your ways with vague apologies;

Pray the Men of Mars to descend upon you. Pray Jehovah to send his prophets before the avenging fire. Pray for second sight and the inner ear. Pray for bulwark against poaching patterns of dislocated days; pray for buttressing iron against insidious termite and beetle and locust and flies and lice and moth and rust and mold.

Part Two

MOLLY MEANS

Old Molly Means was a hag and a witch;
Chile of the devil, the dark, and sitch.
Her heavy hair hung thick in ropes
And her blazing eyes was black as pitch.
Imp at three and wench at 'leben
She counted her husbands to the number seben.
   O Molly, Molly, Molly Means
   There goes the ghost of Molly Means.

Some say she was born with a veil on her face
So she could look through unnatchal space
Through the future and through the past
And charm a body or an evil place
And every man could well despise
The evil look in her coal black eyes.
   Old Molly, Molly, Molly Means
   Dark is the ghost of Molly Means.

And when the tale begun to spread
Of evil and of holy dread:
Her black-hand arts and her evil powers
How she cast her spells and called the dead,
The younguns was afraid at night
And the farmers feared their crops would blight.
   Old Molly, Molly, Molly Means
   Cold is the ghost of Molly Means.

Then one dark day she put a spell
On a young gal-bride just come to dwell
In the lane just down from Molly's shack
And when her husband come riding back
His wife was barking like a dog
And on all fours like a common hog.
   O Molly, Molly, Molly Means
   Where is the ghost of Molly Means?

The neighbors come and they went away
And said she'd die before break of day
But her husband held her in his arms
And swore he'd break the wicked charms;
He'd search all up and down the land
And turn the spell on Molly's hand.
   O Molly, Molly, Molly Means
   Sharp is the ghost of Molly Means.

So he rode all day and he rode all night
And at the dawn he come in sight
Of a man who said he could move the spell
And cause the awful thing to dwell
On Molly Means, to bark and bleed
Till she died at the hands of her evil deed.
   Old Molly, Molly, Molly Means
   This is the ghost of Molly Means.

Sometimes at night through the shadowy trees
She rides along on a winter breeze.
You can hear her holler and whine and cry.
Her voice is thin and her moan is high,
And her cackling laugh or her barking cold
Bring terror to the young and old.
   O Molly, Molly, Molly Means
   Lean is the ghost of Molly Means.

BAD-MAN STAGOLEE*

That Stagolee was an all-right lad
Till he killed a cop and turned out bad,
Though some do say to this very day
He killed more'n one 'fore he killed that 'fay.
But anyhow the tale ain't new
How Stagolee just up and slew
A big policeman on 'leventh street
And all he knowed was tweet-tweet-tweet.
Oh I 'speck he'd done some too-bad dirt
Wid dat blade he wore unnerneaf his shirt
And it ain't been said, but he coulda had
A dirk in his pocket 'cause he sho was bad.
But one thing's certain and two things's sho
His bullets made holes no doc could cyo.
And that there cop was good and done
When he met Stagolee and that blue boy's gun.
But the funniest thing about that job
Was he never got caught by no mob
And he missed the lynching meant for his hide
'Cause nobody knows how Stagolee died.
Bad-man Stagolee ain't no more
But his ghost still walks up and down the shore
Of Old Man River round New Orleans
With her gumbo, rice, and good red beans!

* Pronounced Stack'-a-lee.

POPPA CHICKEN

Poppa was a sugah daddy
Pimping in his prime;
All the gals for miles around
Walked to Poppa's time.

Poppa Chicken owned the town,
Give his women hell;
All the gals on Poppa's time
Said that he was swell.

Poppa's face was long and black;
Poppa's grin was broad.
When Poppa Chicken walked the streets
The gals cried Lawdy! Lawd!

Poppa Chicken made his gals
Toe his special line:
"Treat 'em rough and make 'em say
Poppa Chicken's fine!"

Poppa Chicken toted guns;
Poppa wore a knife.
One night Poppa shot a guy
Threat'ning Poppa's life.

Poppa done his time in jail
Though he got off light;
Bought his pardon in a year;
Come back out in might.

Poppa walked the streets this time,
Gals around his neck.
And everybody said the jail
Hurt him nary speck.

Poppa smoked his long cigars—
Special Poppa brands—
Rocks all glist'ning in his tie;
On his long black hands.

Poppa lived without a fear;
Walked without a rod.
Poppa cussed the coppers out;
Talked like he was God.

Poppa met a pretty gal;
Heard her name was Rose;
Took one look at her and soon
Bought her pretty clothes.

One night she was in his arms,
In walked her man Joe.
All he done was look and say,
"Poppa's got to go."

Poppa Chicken still is hot
Though he's old and gray,
Walking round here with his gals
Pimping every day.

KISSIE LEE

Toughest gal I ever did see
Was a gal by the name of Kissie Lee;
The toughest gal God ever made
And she drew a dirty, wicked blade.

Now this here gal warn't always tough
Nobody dreamed she'd turn out rough
But her Grammaw Mamie had the name
Of being the town's sin and shame.

When Kissie Lee was young and good
Didn't nobody treat her like they should
Allus gettin' beat by a no-good shine
An' allus quick to cry and whine.

Till her Grammaw said, "Now listen to me,
I'm tiahed of yoah whinin', Kissie Lee.
People don't never treat you right,
An' you allus scrappin' or in a fight.

"Whin I was a gal wasn't no soul
Could do me wrong an' still stay whole.
Ah got me a razor to talk for me
An' aftah that they let me be."

Well Kissie Lee took her advice
And after that she didn't speak twice
'Cause when she learned to stab and run
She got herself a little gun.

And from that time that gal was mean,
Meanest mama you ever seen.
She could hold her likker and hold her man
And she went thoo life jus' raisin' san'.

One night she walked in Jim's saloon
And seen a guy what spoke too soon;
He done her dirt long time ago
When she was good and feeling low.

Kissie bought her drink and she paid her dime
Watchin' this guy what beat her time
And he was making for the outside door
When Kissie shot him to the floor.

Not a word she spoke but she switched her blade
And flashing that lil ole baby paid:
Evvy livin' guy got out of her way
Because Kissie Lee was drawin' her pay.

She could shoot glass doors offa the hinges,
She could take herself on the wildest binges.
And she died with her boots on switching blades
On Talladega Mountain in the likker raids.

YALLUH HAMMUH

Old Yalluh Hammuh were a guy
I knowed long time ago.
I seen him pile the san'bags high
An' holler back fuh moah.

I seen him come on inta town
Many a Saddy night
Ridin' high with his jive
An' clownin' leff an' right.

They wasn't no sheriffs near or far
Would dare to 'rest dat man;
An' las' I heerd they wanted him
For two-t'ree county cans.

Old Yalluh Hammuh lay his jive
On mens on every side
And when it come to women folks
His fame was far and wide.

Now Yalluh Hammuh was so bad
He killed his Maw of fright
He swaggered through the county seat
All full of lip and might.

But Yalluh Hammuh met his match
One Saddy night, they say,
He come in town an' run into
Pick-Ankle's gal named May.

Pick-Ankle now was long and lean
An' some say he was mean,
An' if you touched his brown gal, May,
His eyes turned fairly green.

Well this time Yalluh Hammuh's jive
Went to town wid his pay;
He went on in a lil shindig
An' spied Pick-Ankle's May.

He ax huh to dance; she excep;
And then he went to town.
The crowd went wild till here come Pick
And then they quieted down.

But Yalluh Hammuh don't ketch on
Ole May was having fun
Till Pick comes up and calls huh names
Then Yalluh drawed his gun.

The lights went out and womens screamed
And then they fit away.
When Yalluh Hammuh come to hisself
May was gone with his pay.

TWO-GUN BUSTER AND TRIGGER SLIM

Two-Gun Buster was a railroad han'
Splittin' ties in the backwoods lan'
Cuttin' logs and layin' down rails,
Blazin' out the iron horse trails.

Biggest bluff an' cockiest cuss
Two-Gun never had no fuss
'Cause all the hands was frightened dead
At Two-Gun's handy way with lead.

Two-Gun Buster got his fame
Same sorter way he got his name
Carryin' them two guns in his ves'
An' scarin' all the mens at mess.

He had a belly he couldn't fill
With what the cook had on the bill
An' wasn't no second plates allowed
So Two-Gun had the mens all cowed.

An' when he finished with his grub
He made the rest fill up his tub.
He riz and opened up his ves'
An' walked the tables in the mess.

The mens drawed back an' give in to him
Until the Lil Lad cured his whim
'Cause then when Two-Gun started his stuff
That Lil Lad just called his bluff.

Lil Lad looked as green as grass
But he had nerve like brazen brass;
He split them ties like kin'lin' wood.
He sho did earn his plate of food.

At supper time he looked around
When suddenly there warnt a sound
Two-Gun Buster was eatin' a bait
Comin' on down to Lil Lad's plate.

He stuck his fork in Lil Lad's meat
An' Lil Lad rose right to his feet
He grabbed old Two-Gun in a vise
An' axed his meanin' in that wise.

Two-Gun went to draw his steel
But Lil Lad shot him in a reel
Sprawlin' on the mess hall floor
An' all the mens falls out the door.

Lil Lad finish his dinner plate
An' walks on through the camp's big gate;
Don't say no word, an' stayed away;
He didn't come back to draw his pay.

But from that time they made a claim
That they had heerd of him
So they give the Lil Lad a name
And they called him Trigger Slim.

TEACHER

The Teacher was a bad man
   Not a milky-mild
Student with a book or rule
   Punishing a child.

Teacher was a pimp, a rake;
   Teacher was a card.
Teacher had a gambling den
   Down on St. Girod.

Teacher liked his liquor strong;
   Drank his dry gin straight.
Teacher hung around the Tracks
   Catching juicy bait.

Teacher was as black as Aces
   Of a brand new spade.
Teacher's lust included all
   Women ever made.

Teacher's women drove him nuts;
   Led him such a chase
He was stealing extra cash
   For each pretty face.

Women scarred his upper lip;
   Nearly tore his head
Off his shoulders with a gun
   Kept his eyes blood-red.

Women sent him to his doom.
   Women set the trap.
Teacher was a bad, bold man
   Lawd, but such a sap!

GUS, THE LINEMAN

Gus, the lineman,
Route forty-nine;
Our smartest guy
Had a smart line.

He had nine lives
And lived them all.
He climbed the trees
From Fall to Fall.

He handled juice
Whistling a tune;
Chewed tobacco
And drank bad moon . . .

Once on his job
Pains in his side
Said call the doc
Or take a ride.

And in the Ward
They said his side
Was so bad off
He should have died.

But Gus come through
Living the Life
Back on the job
'Spite of that knife.

The juice went wild
And great big chunks
Of flesh caught fire
And fell in hunks.

But Gus outlived
That little fire.
He soon was back
Handling live wire.

It got around
Gus could not die
He'd lived through death
And come through fire.

One Saddy night
Old Gus got high
Drinking moonshine
And good old Rye.

He staggered home
In pitch-black night
And swayed along
From left to right.

He fell into
A little crick
And went out dead
Just like a brick.

They found him drowned
Face in the stream
A cup of water
And his drunk dream.

And thus went down
A mighty guy—
Gus, the lineman,
Who could not die.

LONG JOHN NELSON AND
SWEETIE PIE

Long John Nelson and Sweetie Pie
Lived together on Center Street.
Long John was a mellow fellow
And Sweetie Pie was fat and sweet.

Long John Nelson had been her man
Long before this story began;
Sweetie cooked on the Avenue.
Long John's loving was all he'd do.

When Sweetie Pie came home at night
She brought his grub and fed him well
Then she would fuss and pick a fight
Till he beat her and gave her hell.

She would cuss and scream, call him black
Triflin' man git outa my sight;
Then she would love him half the night
And when he'd leave she'd beg him back.

Till a yellow gal came to town
With coal black hair and bright blue gown
And she took Long John clean away
From Sweetie Pie one awful day.

Sweetie begged him to please come back
But Long John said, "I'm gone to stay."
Then Sweetie Pie would moan and cry
And sing the blues both night and day:

"Long John, Baby, if you'll come back
I won't never call you black;
I'll love you long and love you true
And I don't care what else you do."

But Long John said, "I'm really through."
They're still apart this very day.
When Long John got a job to do
Sweetie got sick and wasted away.

Then after she had tried and tried
One day Sweetie just up and died.
Then Long John went and quit his job
And up and left his yellow bride.

BIG JOHN HENRY

This here's a tale of a sho-nuff man
Whut lived one time in the delta lan'.
His hand was big as a hog's fat ham
And he useta work for Uncle Sam.
His gums was blue, his voice was mellow
And he talked to mules, fellow to fellow.
The day he was born in the Mississippi bottom
He made a meal on buttermilk and sorghum
A mess o' peas and a bait o' tunnips
And when he finished he smacked his lips
And went outside to help pick cotton.
And he growed up taller than a six-foot shooter
Skinnin' mules and catchin' barracuda
And stronger than a team of oxen
And he even could beat the champion boxin'
An' ain't nary man in Dixie's forgotten
How he could raise two bales of cotton
While one hand anchored down the steamboat.
Oh, they ain't no tale was ever wrote
'Bout Big John Henry that could start to tell
All the things that Big Boy knowed so well:
How he learned to whistle from the whippoorwills,
And turned the wheels whut ran the mills;
How the witches taught him how to cunjer,
And cyo the colic and ride the thunder;
And how he made friends with a long lean houn'
Sayin', "It's jes' John Henry a-giftin' 'roun'."
But a ten-poun' hammer done ki-ilt John Henry
Yeah, a ten-poun' hammer ki-ilt John Henry,
Bust him open, wide Lawd!
Drapped him ovah, wide Lawd!
Po' John Henry, he cold and dead.

Part Three

CHILDHOOD

When I was a child I knew red miners
dressed raggedly and wearing carbide lamps.
I saw them come down red hills to their camps
dyed with red dust from old Ishkooda mines.
Night after night I met them on the roads,
or on the streets in town I caught their glance;
the swing of dinner buckets in their hands,
and grumbling undermining all their words.

I also lived in low cotton country
where moonlight hovered over ripe haystacks,
or stumps of trees, and croppers' rotting shacks
with famine, terror, flood, and plague near by;
where sentiment and hatred still held sway
and only bitter land was washed away.

WHORES

When I grew up I went away to work
where painted whores were fascinating sights.
They came on like whole armies through the nights—
their sullen eyes on mine, their mouths a smirk,
and from their hands keys hung suggestively.
Old women working by an age-old plan
to make their bread in ways as best they can
would hobble past and beckon tirelessly.

Perhaps one day they'll all die in the streets
or be surprised by bombs in each wide bed;
learning too late in unaccustomed dread
that easy ways, like whores on special beats,
no longer have the gift to harbor pride
or bring men peace, or leave them satisfied.

IOWA FARMER

I talked to a farmer one day in Iowa.
We looked out far over acres of wheat.
He spoke with pride and yet not boastfully;
he had no need to fumble for his words.
He knew his land and there was love for home
within the soft serene eyes of his son.
His ugly house was clean against the storm;
there was no hunger deep within the heart
nor burning riveted within the bone,
but here they ate a satisfying bread.
Yet in the Middle West where wheat was plentiful;
where grain grew golden under sunny skies
and cattle fattened through the summer heat
I could remember more familiar sights.

MEMORY

I can remember wind-swept streets of cities
on cold and blustery nights, on rainy days;
heads under shabby felts and parasols
and shoulders hunched against a sharp concern;
seeing hurt bewilderment on poor faces,
smelling a deep and sinister unrest
these brooding people cautiously caress;
hearing ghostly marching on pavement stones
and closing fast around their squares of hate.
I can remember seeing them alone,
at work, and in their tenements at home.
I can remember hearing all they said:
their muttering protests, their whispered oaths,
and all that spells their living in distress.

OUR NEED

If dead men died abruptly by a blow—
startled and trapped in today's immediacy,
having neither moments to speak dazedly
nor whimper wistfully—how can they know
or tell us now the way which we should go?
What price upon their wisdom can we stake
if ultimately we would live, not break
beneath a swift and dangerous undertow?

We need a wholeness born of inner strength:
sharp thinking running through our stream of days,
having certain courage flame with honest rays
like slaps of life along the body's length.
We need the friendly feel of human forms
and earth beneath our feet against the storms.

THE STRUGGLE STAGGERS US

Our birth and death are easy hours, like sleep
and food and drink. The struggle staggers us
for bread, for pride, for simple dignity.
And this is more than fighting to exist;
more than revolt and war and human odds.
There is a journey from the me to you.
There is a journey from the you to me.
A union of the two strange worlds must be.

Ours is a struggle from a too-warm bed;
too cluttered with a patience full of sleep.
Out of this blackness we must struggle forth;
from want of bread, of pride, of dignity.
Struggle between the morning and the night.
This marks our years; this settles, too, our plight.

PUBLISHER'S NOTE

THE *Yale Series of Younger Poets* is designed to afford a publishing medium for the work of young men and women who have not yet secured wide public recognition. It will include only verse which seems to give good promise for the future of American poetry—to the development of which it is hoped that the Series may prove a stimulus. Communications concerning manuscripts should be addressed to the Editor of The Yale Series of Younger Poets, in care of the Yale University Press, New Haven, Connecticut.

VOLUMES ALREADY ISSUED